Living Just Now Moments

Decoding the principles of the soul in human life's journey

Daniel A. Dapaah

ISBN: 9798815797659

TABLE OF CONTENTS

Decoding the principles of the soul in human life's journey

Living Just Now Moments

INTRODUCTION

This book has been written with a tone that intends to introduce the reader to develop a keen interest in spirituality and more specifically to discover and acknowledge oneself as a spiritual being with entity attachments that supply life force energies for development and growth.

Everything in life is connected under a neutralised nature environment consisting of plants, animals, and human beings who have been given free will power to choose and seek balance between their good and bad behaviours for stability. For this reason, life purposely creates illusions in different parts of their experiences for them to practically learn the good use of free will power and try to seek the right path to redeem and set the soul free from the bondage of darkness. Souls may represent the immortal light creatures who travel down to earth in the energy form of light and darkness. They purposely come to inhabit mortal human beings for a life – changing experiences in several human incarnations to purge out the negative influences of the dark side and reform to become divine creatures.

When mortal human beings are under the negative influences of the dark soul, they tend to live superficial lifestyles to generally please the lower ego – self. This is a typical personality that most likely gets them drawn to worldly pleasures because of a mentally developed hypersensitive sense of self – importance that is often constructed for the sake of the status quo within one's community or the societal groups they follow. Somehow it has led to the loss of the fundamental meaning of life and the purpose of mankind's existence as a multidimensional being with limitless spiritual possibilities in a physical presence to transform and evolve.

Once mankind finally evolves and reaches the higher heights in their vibrational state of consciousness, they automatically gain access to new knowledge and understanding about creation and human life through divine guidance from the enhanced intuition they develop with the deeper connection between source energy and the frequency of God. From then onwards, life in the physical world becomes promising and much brighter because of the clarity brought in by the positive blend and appropriate balance between the dual spiritual and physical nature of human existence.

CHAPTER 1 – THE STORYLINE

Once upon a time in a faraway super – advanced world, there lived a group of immortal supernatural beings of light who lived faithful and just amongst themselves through the impressive qualities of uprightness, fairness, loyalty, and unconditional love. One day, they decided to grow and expand their kingdom whilst still maintaining these qualities and magnificent standards that they have kept for eons of light – years. So, they came up with a plan to create beings who would have to go through development and training to evolve and become like their calibre.

In an attempt to do this, they sorted out various strategies and also considered a means by which these created beings would taste and experience sin. But their main concern was to find a way to prevent the destruction that it could cause from entering their beautiful kingdom. As a result of that, they invented the universe or a miniature kingdom to theirs for the mass production of mortal human beings who would become hosts to take the immortal light beings through their series of developmental training and reformation processes with the various kinds of energetic information that would be presented to them by the creator. The programme is also intended to take the mortal human being through different growth stages and transformation to develop a mindset of good moral standing and dignity.

So, the plan kicked – off with the creation of the "soul". This is the energetic version of the immortal light beings that would reside in an invisible dimensional state to the mortal human beings. This dimensional state of existence may also be referred to as the spiritual world or the unseen inner – world of mortal human beings. The Spiritual world is assumed to contain a huge data bank consisting of various types and forms of energy to manage and regulate all the different kinds and states of matter objects in the mortal human beings' universe.

These energies move in waves of vibration at either low or high – frequency rates whereby the low – frequency spectrum circulates negative energies, and the high – frequency on the hand circulates positive energies. This energetic flow state may also describe the spiritual soul as having a dual opposite light and dark sides to define the core and complete makeup of mortal human beings. The light side which may also be presented as the "Higher self" could be described as the advanced and highly evolved nature of mortal human beings. This part generally influences positive actions and good deeds whereas the opposite dark counterpart that represents the "Lower self" occupies the low frequency area with negative energies to encourage bad deeds and evil actions.

These two main sides of the spiritual soul could also be perceived as the direct channels that allow life force energies to flow into mortal human beings to direct their life experiences. Meanwhile, the Creator's idea for the dual design of the spiritual soul is for mortal human beings to live and experience both sides so that they may try to seek a suitable balance that most likely has the light higher self attaining greater power of influence to overcome the evil tendencies of the dark lower self. This in the end introduces the true nature of "God" within the spiritual soul to influence mortal human beings to adapt and keep the good and righteous ways of living as an integral part of their existence.

CHAPTER 2 – CONCEPTS OF THE INNER WORLD OR SPIRITUAL DIMENSION

A – THE CREATOR OF THE UNIVERSE

The physical appearance or true identity of the creator is yet to be confirmed but to the best of human knowledge, the creator may be described as some "Supreme" immortal light beings. Although their nature of existence may be foreign and invisibly outside the scope of the mortal human kingdom, they contribute a lot to the physical realities of human life. They are in fact super – intelligent and highly advanced beings who live eons of light – years beyond the solar system at a place mostly referred to as the "Heavens" or Paradise. Collectively, they form a set of male and female righteous beings who live in cities far ahead in civilisation and technology as compared to the human world. There have also been some speculations about their existence here on earth centuries of years ago with the paramount importance of beginning the human race before departing.

B – THE KINGDOM OF LIGHT (HEAVEN OR PARADISE)

The Kingdom of light, Heaven, or Paradise as it may be referred to, is known to be a celestial world and a home for all righteous souls who greatly honour the divine virtues of goodness, fairness, and uprightness. It is a highly developed serene dwelling place for the Creator and all evolved souls who once went through earth life's training to ascend and inherit their rightful places in the Kingdom. It is also where immortal light beings are created and teleported as energy to inhabit mortal human beings for the exploration of human life on earth to reform. Moreover, the reformative process may require the completion of several human life lessons and gradually progress through various transitional stages of living in the dark and eventually into the light to ascend back to the Kingdom.

C – THE SPIRITUAL SOUL

Up in the heavens, immortal light beings are created by the supreme beings of the light. They then put them into a deep sleep of hibernation in chambers containing a technological time travel system that teleports or transports them into the miniature world of mortal human beings to represent the soul in light energy form. Activities in the human world generally transpire between the dual realities of the spiritual and physical dimensional states or realms whereby operations in the spiritual realm mostly involve unseen forces or entities that transmit negative or positive energies at frequencies of low and high rates respectively.

The physical realm, on the other hand, handles and presents all the visible activities including the physical existence of creatures like mortal human beings. It is usually supported by universal life forces of light and darkness that supply energies in positive (+) and negative (-) polarities through the spiritual soul to regulate all the physical activities including the events in human life. In other translations, the soul may be seen as the gateway or portal that juggles between two opposite life force energies to allow mortal human beings to have access to different kinds of energetic information that are stored up in the energetic data bank or the psyche of the subconscious part of the human brain which may be located somewhere up above so high in the skies or the stars.

The energetic data bank is basically a storage system that stores a collection of energetic information that could be accessed to reconstruct or rebuild mortal human beings to evolve with better attributes and also be able to refine broken fragments of their nature, especially in the following aspects;

- The self – aspect involving individuality and gender specification
- The Behavioural aspect of good moral stances and character development
- The social aspect involving individualistic interactions and positive impact on society
- The physical aspect of recreating a healthy and durable body for endurance, stability, and longevity
- The emotional aspect which involves the ability to develop and express genuine love, compassion, and empathy for individual self and fellow humankind
- The spiritual aspect that entails knowing and acknowledging the dual light and dark nature of the soul and its essence in human life experiences
- The mental aspect of seeking the appropriate balance between life force energies for a meaningful life experience

Energies in the spiritual soul's data bank are purposely selected by the creator to generate the genetic codes that form the birth of mortal human beings. But these pieces of genetic information may often contain imperfections or a lot of broken data that may challenge physical growth and the tendencies of developing good character and moral standards for the enlightenment goals. Therefore, spiritual souls end up undergoing a series of human lifetime lessons to reform by transmuting the bad energies to repair the broken genetic data. In the background, the process recalibrates the plus (+) and minus (-) strands of the DNA for a potential increase in the plus (+) or high vibrational energies that may be capable of fixing the broken fragments within the energetic arrangement of the spiritual soul.

When the soul's data bank has completely reformed to a

divine standard after several human lifetimes, it triggers its release from the earth's life cycle and returns to the kingdom of light or the source to supply or feed the immortal light being.

D – CHARACTERISTICS OF THE SOUL

The characteristics of the spiritual soul may physically be seen in the outward projection of the mortal human being's lifestyle which may portray either good or bad behavioural traits to represent the light and dark sides of the energy supply from universal life forces.

The physical world of mortal human beings may actually be perceived as engulfed by an electromagnetic field that produces energetic light souls. The soul is also thought to be pre – programmed with universal life forces or unseen entities that supply energies for regulation and human transformation. So as the process turns out to reform the energies within the soul, the light side begins to shine brighter through the behavioural patterns of the mortal human being with the newly improved energetic arrangement. In this respect, mortal human beings may be classified as bodysuits or vessels for souls to inhabit with spiritual entities to control and manage mortal human life to evolve the soul for the better.

The soul may have also been designed with a receptor – like feature to allow a two – way communication or the exchange of energy signals. This tends to allow outside influences from external forces that may include fellow humankind. It may also allow the communication between mortal human beings and the creator a better chance for monitoring growth levels as the soul transitions gradually through the two distinct self – states designed for the human developmental and evolutionary project for enlightenment.

The Higher and Lower Self States

The higher – self, has a purpose or mission that influences mortal human beings to live in compassion, goodness, and kindness towards fellow human beings and other creatures as opposed to the lower – self or dark counterpart whose mission may be depicted as the reverse with huge influences and supply of low vibrational energies to dominate and control the mind with evil thoughts and activities. But somehow the initial structure of the component that underpins the composition of the mortal body vessel automatically selects the lower – self as the primitive state for a majority of mortal human beings. This primary component of the body vessel is made up of atoms which are the fundamental building materials found in various states of matter whether solid, liquid, gas, or plasma type of object. Atoms have a basic structure consisting of a central nucleus containing a positive electrical field of protons and zero – electric charged neutrons to provide extra stability within the nucleus. The nucleus is also surrounded by a large electrical field of negative electrons that orbit around in shells. These electrical fields within an atom are mostly the composition of chemical elements with either positive or negative ions.

Atomic ions create bonds to form cells that develop various organ systems to regulate the mortal body vessel. These cells have barriers with a semi – permeable membrane that functions by a selective type of regulation to control the substances that enter and go out of the cell. This may also mean that the barriers may allow certain types of substances to pass through whiles restricting or blocking entry for other types. Therefore, if the default settings of the barriers in the human cells are set to restrict the inflow of positive ions, there would definitely be an influx of negative ions and in summary, this may suggest or contribute to the reasons why the interim formation of the mortal body vessel may be dense and highly susceptible to influences from low vibrational energies which in turn negatively affects human actions and activities. This kind of setup often suppresses or totally rejects energetic signals from light sources therefore it causes mortal human beings to hide behind a personality trait that is masked with false pretences and commonly associated with bad and evil practices.

Such a faulty constructed personality is commonly referred to as the "Ego". It is closely tied up to living an extra selfish or self – absorbed lifestyle that tends to avoid expressing love, compassion, and empathy to others apart from oneself. The ego may considerably be quite a deceptive human nature that mostly thrives with the prompts of the dark lower – self. It is also highly fickle and mainly focuses on superficial lifestyles because it depends mostly on social approval to gain power and control over others. It tends to do all of that due to the fear of being naturally authentic to consciously choose to improve and live by the mission of the higher – self. But after the lower self or dark soul has gone through various human life lessons and experiences, positive changes cause recalibration in the internal atomic structure and allow the new arrangement to bring in positive influences through the light part of the soul and other external light sources to affect how much of the ego drives the mortal human being.

Free Will Power

The mortal body vessel had "free will" power incorporated as an important mechanism to direct the flow of the dual life force energy supply that comes through the soul. Moreover, the creator prefers that mortal human beings may live independently and be free to choose or pursue their heart desires and ambitions in life. But unfortunately, the desires of man often suffer from a lack of self – discipline or self – control which often leads to choosing wrongful desires that may tie in with various evil acts.

Therefore, the need to monitor free will choices with close vigilance and moral justification may be quite important for mortal human beings to thrive and succeed in life because the human world was purposely built with the inclusion of sin and evil acts to test mankind. Another important essence of free will in human design is for mortal human beings to have the power to control and regulate all conscious decisions which in turn allows mortal human beings to choose which part of the soul's energy supply may have the most dominance over their actions or activities. Meanwhile, free will power is assumed to handle 10% of all conscious reasoning and decision making in the complete regulatory processes of mortal human beings whilst almost 90% of the regulation remains involuntary activities held by the subconscious mind. This is where all the pre – programmed templates are stored alongside the spiritual soul.

Producing Light With Atoms

Usually, the changes that happen in the internal structure of the mortal body vessel can best be described by how atoms generate electricity to produce light. This is normally observed as an electric current flow connection between positive and negative ions. However, the brightness and stability of the light may be determined by the flow state or measured by the ratio of charges between the connecting ions that are present in the atom. In that sense, an electron or negative ion may lose a charge within the connection for protons or the positive ions gain the power to increase their charges. Likewise, positive ions may lose charge for negative ions to gain the power to increase the electrical charge. However, electrons or negative ions are mostly known to be unstable due to their free – flow characteristics and weaker bonding properties so they tend to lose charges quite easily within a connection. But positive ions or protons on the other hand create much stronger bonds because they are tightly held together inside the nucleus with neutrons to increase and tighten up the bonds to provide extra stability.

However, the illustration above may lead to describe the configuration setup of two major types of ions known as cation and anion that forms within an atom. Cations form a structure in an atom where there are more protons and a smaller number of electrons to make the atom positively charged. But anions make negatively charged atoms with widespread or more electrons than protons. Therefore, this may imply that by default the initial build of the mortal body vessel may contain a lot of anionic atoms to purposely contribute to its lower vibrational state at the early stages so that life transformational lessons may later cause changes to increase the number of cationic atoms to improve and raise the vibrational frequency within the body vessel higher.

Meanwhile, the result of having this initial low vibrational configuration may also have some poor performance effects on vital organ systems like the brain which sometimes suffer a lot of distortions coming from external influences or bad energies that some fellow humankind may project onto others to limit conscious activities and optimum performance. Another vital organ that may also be affected is the heart which supports brain activities with the circulation of ionic substances or energies around for internal communication to be enhanced and prevent chemical imbalances within the body vessel. Therefore, circulating bad energies may certainly affect chemical reactions and lead to body malfunctioning. But somehow the situation may recover with individual efforts to self – improve and allow the positive changes to bad behaviours and other unhealthy lifestyles also cause effective changes to the atomic and cellular framework through the transmutational processes that may be occurring behind the scenes. Therefore, it may be a key suggestion for every individual to try and seek to focus on the life lessons that have been uniquely assigned for their personal growth. Because it could effectively have the body (mortal vessel), mind (consciousness), and soul (life forces) aligned for better coordination to improve physical, mental, and spiritual maturity as expected.

Soul Pairing

Souls are mostly created in pairs purposely for unions or partnerships later on in the human life on earth and beyond as divine partners or kingdom spouses after they have returned back home for eternal life. However, each pair goes through their own separate earth life training to develop and evolve independently because the assignments are essentially created to allow them to explore and learn more about the different aspects of the masculine and feminine energies in regard to gender goals and preferences. This process often takes many long years and lifetimes to explore life between the two main human genders to clearly understand the responsibilities and unique roles that may be assigned to both genders. This also gives each soul pair the opportunity to try and seek a suitable balance between the masculine and feminine energies present in each of them and be able to personally select a dominant one to match their gender preferences. Afterward, the information may then be stored in the psyche or subconscious mind to redefine the immortal light being later.

Once these half – souls reach a certain tipping point on their journeys, they are brought together through the creator's design into a final human lifetime where they get to meet and try to merge through a divinely guided awakening process. This process is specifically designed to allow each of them to go against the odds and overcome various obstacles to clear out past life issues or karma. It may also involve some other forms of restrictions that may result from childhood programming in the current lifetime that may tend to hinder the chances of them coming together and merge their half – souls to become a complete whole alpha – male and omega – female divine partners here on earth before they depart to become kingdom spouses in the afterlife.

Gender Preferences

The gender preferences chapter in the human life experiences forms an integral part of the soul's journey to allow each soul pair to personally define its preferred gender. It also establishes within the soul's energetic framework a suitable balance between the masculine and feminine energies that are both present in each pair and may both likely have weaknesses (negative) and strengths (positive) associated with them.

The masculine energies mostly carry the attributes of a man or the male hormonal properties and characteristics while the feminine carries female hormonal properties and characteristics. They are both ideally supposed to be expressed to match the corresponding physical appearance or body type of mortal human beings. Therefore, the appropriate expression order for the masculine and feminine energies of each of the two genders is for the men or males to express more of the masculine energies that contain the hormonal properties called progesterone than the female hormonal properties. And likewise, the female counterparts are also expected to express more feminine energies containing the hormonal property, oestrogen more than progesterone which may be commonly high in the men.

In some exceptional cases, the feminine or masculine energies may express more than necessary in the wrong physical body type, and in such instances, the female person may have more progesterone hormone expressed to make them exhibit some sort of masculine tendencies or a man may end up having more oestrogen expressed to cause them to develop certain female features and may even portray some female – like gestures and behaviours. However, these are common imbalances that occur to bring to attention the need for individual souls to evolve and correctly balance out their masculine and feminine energies so that they may be properly expressed as the human life journey progresses.

In two different highlights, the table below shows some basic personality traits that are often displayed by the masculine and feminine genders which may be evaluated to give better stances and improve on these common gender behaviours. For instance, a man harbouring aggressive tendencies may want to improve and emphasise authority as a positive alternative to deflect such negative traits. But then sometimes certain circumstances may force the use of negative traits to handle situations smoothly. Therefore, the goal should actually be to evaluate and choose traits that best suit or seems to handle situations much better.

Masculine		Feminine	
Weakness (-)	Strength (+)	Weakness (-)	Strength (+)
Aggressive	Authoritative	Insecure	Humility
Dominant	Gentle	Obsessive	Caring
Violent	Protective	Frightened	Empathetic
Egotistical	Goal – Oriented	Fragile	Stylish or Attractive
Argumentative	Action Oriented	Complaining	Highly Communicative
Self – importance	Confidence	Inquisitive	Discerning
Pride	Dignity	Indecisive	Careful
Defiant	Resilience	Shy or Timid	Considerate

E – THE SOUL'S JOURNEY

The journey normally begins at the dark soul level or the lower frequency state of mortal human beings before a gradual transition into higher frequency states occurs with the life lessons that may transpire as temptations, obstacles, and challenges. It may also be considered as a gradual shift from darkness into the space of light and allow positive influences to flow into the consciousness of mortal human beings to affect and improve their decision – making and activities.

The Human Life Experience

All the events and scenarios in human life may be centred around pre – written storylines containing different characters with various lifestyles and associated responsibilities for mortal human beings to act and evolve. Therefore, each individual person may form part of several small cast groups or soul family groups consisting of direct family members, friends, spouses or partners, neighbours, work colleagues as well as certain animals or pets. They have all been assigned specific roles that fit into the overall big picture that is intended for the mass collective growth and transitioning through various stages in life to eventually embody the higher consciousness of the soul.

The human life experiences may unfold and spread across several earthly lifetimes or evolutionary phases. Each evolutionary phase may differ because the roles and scenarios may change to complement the life's purpose in that particular lifetime. This could be emphasising certain important aspects like character development or healing from bad habits and behaviours to evolve and be able to progress forward onto the next phase. The experiences in human life may play an important role to cause the human lower self state or self – made ego personality to eventually dissolve and allow the development of a higher personality that is in the likeness of "God".

God is a concept that may represent the predetermined nature of the soul which acknowledges and seeks proper balance between the light (high frequency) and darkness (low frequency) in a ratio that gives much dominance to the light or "**Goodness** to **Overrule Darkness**" **(God).** Balancing the energies within the soul may seem quite essential in human life because the dark soul may be affiliated with low vibrational entities that may also represent demonic agents whose main intentions are to influence mortal human beings to bring pain and misery to fellow humankind through causing havoc and chaotic situations. But the high vibrational or light soul may represent the opposite because the angelic team has pure intentions that influence goodness and uprightness so that peace and love may prevail amongst all humanity.

Universal life forces, in general, may be involved with unseen creatures or entities that transmit high and low energies through frequency channels or portal openings within the soul. This in human life experiences officially creates a split spread of collective groups of bad low vibrational people (villains) and good high vibrational people (heroes) who may find themselves in a strike battle for power and dominance to control the physical world and all humanity. Meanwhile, the expected goal for this arrangement is to have a majority of humankind follow or become angelic crew members and be on a high vibration to win this spiritual battle against the low vibrational dark forces for God to reign in larger parts of the earth.

CHAPTER 3 – CONCEPTS OF THE OUTER WORLD OR PHYSICAL DIMENSION

A – THE KINGDOM OF DARKNESS (PLANET EARTH)

Planet earth in the solar system was created as a habitat to nurture and influence growth for various kinds of creatures and organisms in creation or nature. It is also intended to mimic the living conditions and standards that are similar to the heavens so that humankind may live in peace and harmony instead of the current broken living state that mostly encourages and supports dangerous activities patronised through various dark avenues for survival means and purposes.

Normal life on earth involves the dual nature of human existence whereby souls inhabit the human body in a high and low energy state to influence life events. However, the evolution of the soul spreads over a series of lifetimes on earth to progressively reform from the low to high state and have a positive impact on improving the lives of mortal human beings. The assignment may also require mortal human beings to use their freewill power for conscious decision making over the choices made between universal life forces and eventually become enlightened to develop a good demeanour which may come from the programmed lessons that tend to correct previous bad choices and past mistakes done at the dark lower self state.

Earth in another translation may also exist through quantum lenses where it is thought to be enclothed or around an electromagnetic field surrounded by cosmic bodies transmitting life force energies at variable frequency rates. The energies may normally spread across a cluster of positive and negative polarity fields where the negative field area may be spiritually assigned to demonic entities or the dark forces that encourage evil practices and bad deeds while the positive energy field on the other hand may spiritually signify angelic entities or light forces that exude high vibrational energies to influence and promote goodness, love, compassion, and kindness amongst humanity and all creatures of the earth.

B – UNIVERSAL LIFE FORCES

A force from a scientific perspective suggests a means tailored to cause action for work to be done and obtain an outcome. Therefore, in the context of creation and human existence, forces represent the energy supply sources that influence mortal human beings to take certain kinds of actions to generate various outcomes. Mortal human beings mainly function in the physical dimensional state of existence with the assistance of the spiritual soul which may also be connected to spiritual entities or life force energies that influence their decisions to result in diverse outcomes. The outcomes, in general, may also imply that, in every action, there is a development of an opposite response or reaction that needs to be endured for certain lessons to be learned.

Forces and Spiritual Entities

Mortal human beings may sometimes label forces as spirits or entity creatures of light and darkness. But then again, spirits may also refer to the creator or the unseen supernatural beings who are involved in the various purposes of regulating and guiding human evolution or creation as a whole. They may exist in various forms in the physical realm and within other planetary bodies of the cosmos at different frequency rates. They may also originate or belong to the following classifications;

Spirits of the Light (Good)

- They represent the kingdom of light and the Most – High or Godly spiritual beings such as the angelic or divine beings, and spiritual guides or guardians
- They support and influence the act of goodness and uprightness
- They are high vibrational creatures or entities

Spirits of Darkness (Bad)

- They represent the kingdom of darkness and the ungodly or dark creatures such as demonic spiritual beings and agents of the devil
- They encourage and influence all evil deeds and bad practices
- They are low vibrational creatures or entities

Both spiritual forces and/or entities transmit their energetic information simultaneously for the mortal human mind to analyse through thought patterns and allow conscious choices to be made with freewill power. But when freewill choices are frequently made under the influences of a particular spiritual source, it tends to create certain deeper connections which then allows the spiritual source to eventually take over and possess the mortal human being to fully control their decisions and actions. Meanwhile, the human project suggests that all humankind may become righteous by collaborating with good spirits whose energy supply may grant them the opportunity to receive divine guidance to positively affect their lives for better outcomes.

C – THE MORTAL HUMAN BEING

Human life began with the creation of immortal light beings up in the Heavens who had to travel to earth in spiritual form as the energetic soul to supply life force energies for mortal human beings to change and become the best versions of themselves. Throughout the transformational process or life of mortal human beings, the immortal light beings stay in hibernation in the Heavens or the light kingdom. This is to allow the energetic soul to conjoin and complete a series of human life lessons in many lifetimes to reform and finally be released out of the earth's life cycles for a return to bring the immortal light being back alive or out of the hibernation.

Zodiac Signs And Human Birth

The soul is basically a product of the electromagnetic field energy of light produced by the sun. It also comprises universal particles of the four basic elements including water, air, earth, and fire that make – up the entire universe. Three of these elements may constitute the fundamental substances behind every creature on the land, sea, and in the atmospheric space of planet earth whiles the fire component in the mix may signify the sun which is the main source of life force energies.

In the infinite wisdom of the creator, the aforementioned elements developed four groups of stars that further created three different variations of each of the four elements to make up twelve constellations. This then became the twelve standard zodiac signs under which mortal human beings and other creatures are born or created on earth.

The Twelve Zodiac Signs			
Air signs	**Earth signs**	**Fire signs**	**Water signs**
Aquarius	Capricorn	Aries	Cancer
Gemini	Taurus	Leo	Pisces
Libra	Virgo	Sagittarius	Scorpio

The twelve zodiac signs may also be seen as a simulation template for the replication of mortal creatures like human beings in the evolutionary project. Each sign consists of unique qualities and personality traits that may define the collective group of mortal human beings who are conceived under the signs to embark on the human life journey to evolve. There are also at least three advancement levels involved with each sign. Therefore, those that are born at the basic level of a sign may be classified as young souls whiles others may be born under the sign at the intermediate or advanced levels depending on how much they have evolved. These cohort groups may be classified or fall under the category of old souls who may have been created earlier and have reincarnated severally to complete many life lessons to advance slightly ahead of the others.

The human evolution project may also be closely monitored and under the vigilance of other planetary bodies or forces that put together life lessons and events and incorporate them into the zodiac signs. These programming may formally be considered as "fated" encounters or predetermined situations that most likely must happen to the collective or individual human being whether good or bad. This energetic data may also include and correspond to the information of the ancestral bloodline genes that mortal human beings may inherit many generations back. Sometimes they may include some exclusive features or factors to distinguish individuals from the collective group. This cud be in the form of certain personality traits or physical form features and even generational curses. In the case of generational curses mortal human beings must be warned and learn to recognise the patterns of these curses so that they may heal to free future generations from inheriting such negative patterns and make life become much easier for them.

Origin Of The Human Race

The past era most likely saw more life within the animal kingdom where early animal creatures may have diversified through a natural selection process to adapt to environmental changes for survival and expansion. But as time went by through different stages of evolution on earth, the initiation of cross – breeding began and brought forth different species like the homo – sapiens and this led to the rise of the human race. This may also imply that centuries of years before human life became popular in existence, ancestral souls inhabited and had to live animal lives until the human race emerged from the homo – sapiens species. Since then, the human race has drastically increased with several reproduction cycles to continue the human evolutionary project and allow mortal human beings to advance logically and intellectually through transformation.

As a result of that, human beings have through the ages of time evolved immensely to increase mental capacity with inclinations in cognitive behaviours and intellectual abilities which has also led to improvements in areas such as socio – economic, scientific, and technological advancements to enhance global connections between humanity. Whilst this may speak of impressive achievements in human relations, other areas may still be lacking due to ancestral or past conflicts which may be preventing peace and unity from existing amongst humanity to allow extensive interactive growth.

This modern era may have a lot to show or teach mortal human beings their connectedness to the same giant pool of life force energies which is basically the sun manifesting with the moon through the soul to create mortal human beings who may come from different backgrounds, race, colour, traditions, and belief systems. Therefore, any sense of separateness is just an illusion to cause division. That is why if the perception of "Oneness" consciousness gets the chance to circulate as a globalised movement, it may brew "One love" amongst humanity and help to dissolve all the old and past conflicts separating mortal human beings from many generations down the line to this present day.

D – THE SOLAR SYSTEM AND OTHER COSMIC BODIES

The solar system may strategically involve certain cosmic planets and other bodies that revolve around the central sun in an interconnected networking system that builds the foundation on which all living and non – living things in the universe get constructed or created.

There are nine basic planets including planet earth that makes up the solar system. Earth was essentially constructed as a habitat with cosmic energetic particles to develop and grow its land, sea, and air – based life forms to thrive through the living conditions it provides for breeding and nurturing various kinds of creatures including human beings who may be harvested by immortal light beings to undergo certain processes to reform. The remaining eight planets bare significant roles in the management and regulation of human life experiences. They may also handle several duties including programming life lessons, events, and challenges that bring about positive changes for mortal human beings to evolve and live a **Life Of Righteous Deeds** (Lord). The term lord then became spiritually honoured and offered to address all the eight planets of the universe or cosmos. The lords of the universe may also be considered as the teachers who run different sections and themes under the human developmental training programme. They may incorporate various life challenges into the soul's programming to allow humankind to exercise their free will power and take certain actions to bring development and growth to their lives. However, these actions may sometimes unravel further difficult challenges that may detour and also prolong the growth processes.

A Brief Role Of The Cosmic Bodies

The sun has a grand role as the main source of life force energies on the planet. It also replenishes and revitalises the soul with sustainable power to manage mortal human beings and other creatures

The moon is a supporting life force energy and may also be responsible for the recycling processes of all organisms and creatures on the planet through birth and rebirth cycles. It may sometimes have some symbolic spiritual linkage to the secrecy and occult knowledge in human life experiences

Mercury may be related to all the logical and intellectual aspects of mortal human beings

Venus may be in charge of areas involving emotional feelings and love affections

Earth exists as a habitat for nurturing and breeding all kinds of creatures in nature

Mars may deal with the development of passion and courage for mortal human life

Jupiter may provide abundance and optimism for expansion in life

Saturn ensures the adherence to discipline and stirs up determination for success in human life

Uranus encourages originality and authenticity in life aspirations and endeavours

Neptune manages all major spiritual matters including subjects like imaginations, intuition, dreams, delusions, and spiritual forces or entities

Pluto may be responsible for regulating regeneration processes, transformation or death and rebirth processes that happen to all the creatures in the universe

E – IMPORTANT ASPECTS IN HUMAN LIFE EXPERIENCES

Human life experiences naturally follow the concept of God which translates into good and bad storylines or events. However, life events may be filled with many illusions that may pretend to be real just to purposely confuse mortal human beings so that they may discern and make informed choices to balance out the universal life force energies. Lifeforce energies often navigate directly through a triad composition of the Body, Mind, and Soul which tends to be the most essential because it consists of the templates that outline the activity layouts and guided reports that potentially bring about positive changes for mortal human beings to advance and evolve. A lot of the illusions in human life may be due to a lack of knowledge and understanding of the duality in life. And it is because mortal human beings usually fail to acknowledge the higher wisdom of the soul and its potential to elevate human consciousness higher to perceive and see past the deceptive veil hovering over major parts of the human life experiences.

For quite some time now mankind's true purpose in life has greatly been distorted by some deceptive focus out of the lack of patience and extreme greed to gain worldly pleasures and material wealth. As a result of that, a majority of mortal human beings end up rushing in life to find easier ways to attain these pleasurable desires for selfish interest and self – gratification. Unfortunately, the result of seeking such desires also attracts short – cut ways to attain them. But they are mostly associated with all sorts of dark and evil means that also have the tendency to put lives at great risk. Moreover, indulging in dangerous activities or lifestyles of any dark form or nature may certainly permit evil dark forces to fully possess the soul and corrupt the mind to control and rule over all of its conscious activities which in turn may lead to destroying personal life and that of others too.

Fate and Destiny

The foundational structure of human life may intertwine between two combined concepts including ***"Fate"*** or divine willpower. This may refer to the predetermined events that are meant to happen or play out in human life regardless of the turn – out of events or situations that may develop along the way to cause hindrances. It may also be considered as a set of positive plans and layouts that are intended to guide and put mankind back on track to be aligned with their true purpose and mission after drifting off their path from outside negative influences. The other structural concept is ***"Destiny"*** which may also tie in with the given freewill power that allows mankind to exercise conscious efforts to either strictly follow the procedures set in the divine will and co – create with the universe or choose to follow a different path. But usually, these alternative paths cause delays to prolong the growth processes. As a matter of fact, lack of knowledge and clarity often makes mortal human beings ignorantly reject the divine path and choose the alternative one because they may seem uncomfortable at first, but it mostly ends with great satisfaction and maturity.

However, a large part of the alternative path mostly feels more comfortable based on human preferences, but they often lack growth and maturity which tends to make it difficult to co – create with the universe and evolve. Because most of the options on this path may be full of temptations to entice mankind and cause them to engage in selfish desires and pleasures that come with no growth and sometimes with catastrophic outcomes. Meanwhile, it is a very common choice or option for most mortal human beings until the difficult situations and uncomfortable lessons sets in and makes them revert back onto the divine path to evolve out of their ignorance and comfort zones.

Freewill and Karma

Freewill then again relates to an individual's own decisions and choices that may result in either a positive or negative outcome. However, the choices and actions in human life may also correlate with the universal laws of karma which state that "all causes have an equal or opposite reaction or effect". This may further imply that every human action and deed done in the past or previously may accumulate and eventually return back many folds as rewards from the universe. This could either be a good or bad reward depending on the sort of karma that has been accumulated and the sort of lesson that the universe wants to emphasise to ensure the right growth outcome for individuals. The karma justice system in creation is basically for the sake of fairness and balance to be maintained within the entire universe and amongst mortal human beings. Therefore, the result of bad karma shouldn't always be negatively perceived as a punishment from the universe or divine spirits. But instead, it may be seen as an opportunity to find balance within the individual self and allow for greater dignity to be observed so that mankind may serve and treat themselves and fellow humankind with much love and respect.

The Human Life Plan

Every mortal human being possesses a life plan that is intended to guide and monitor individual growth processes. They are usually programmed by higher forces of the universe with the intention to evolve mankind's consciousness higher to receive and comprehend high vibrational messages from the universe. Universal messages are generally organised and transmitted through the psyche or subconscious mind – space to influence and bring about the conscious awareness of the high vibrational frequency of God into the life of mortal human beings. Therefore, the creator or higher forces may expect all humankind to eventually embody or tap into this frequency to transform and allow the positive changes to reform the energetic framework of the soul.

Energy Life Span

Energy often lasts with the task embedded into its programming. Therefore, when mankind refuses to use up or make the effort to complete the task like making the necessary changes to transform, higher forces may step in and drastically cause the changes to happen whether they are ready or not to allow the old energies to be used and die out or decay to make room for a new set of energies to come and continue the process. As a matter of fact, energy cannot be destroyed completely but it may undergo transmutation or decay processes to lose or gain potency charges. However, the increment in potency charges may also have a potential effect of transforming mortal human beings to become high vibrational and be able to receive high vibrational messages to improve and become advanced.

Mortal human beings by nature are capable of downloading or receiving universal messages that are within low and high – frequency bandwidth. These signals create different kinds of thought patterns in the mind that may end up developing all sorts of actions. However, the capacity at which the mortal human being can receive and decipher high frequency messages is dependent on the state or level of consciousness. This means that if they have not evolved highly enough and mostly function within lower conscious states, then they may not be able to access high – frequency messages or even comprehend them. The lower state of consciousness may also be a common limiting factor hindering mortal human beings from living their everyday life and activities with the much – needed dignity, values, and greater levels of moral standards. Therefore self – improvement work may generally be required to raise the energetic frequency level within the body, mind, and soul, to become one with the frequency of God which may begin to turn around things and allow divine guidance from higher forces to assist in living a better and meaningful life.

The Aura And Energy Centres

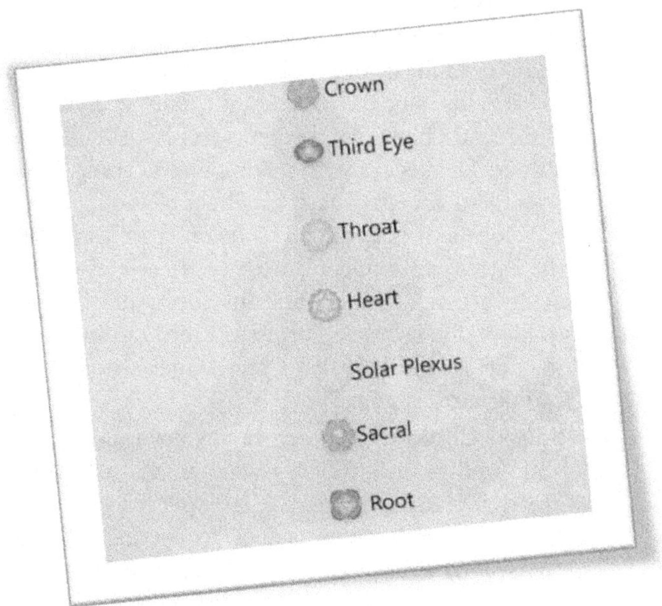

Apart from the body's visible or physical appearance, it may also be connected to some other invisible layers like the emotional body which is integrated into the aura to regulate mood processes that correspond with feelings and emotions. The aura may be considered as an energetic field that operates as a transmitter and receiver component to regulate energy flow within the body vessel. It is also assumed to be wired to seven key energy centres known as "Chakras" which could be found along the spine of mortal human beings.

The chakras may also function by connecting to the main organ systems that make up the internal framework of the body vessel. The connection may begin from the bottom base known as the root chakra to the base on top of the head where the crown chakra sits to create the energetic passageway for communication within and outside the body environment to receive influences and assistance from higher forces of the universe.

- **Root Chakra:** This centre sits at the base of the spine or tailbone area. The energies here are meant to provide signals to feel safe and grounded to withstand challenges and survival issues like being able to feel secure with having and keeping money to afford needs such as shelter and food. Its development is assumed to begin from birth up to the early years of age. But when these early growth stages are met with chaotic environments, they tend to block the correct energy flow into the area which may affect individuals to sometimes develop a lot of insecurities when they get older

- **Sacral Chakra:** This centre sits around the lower abdomen to be affiliated with emotional control, creativity, and sexuality. It is expected to develop from the adolescence stages to the early teenage years. However, it can be blocked due to abuse or trauma which often affects individuals in adulthood with a lack of having control over their own lives which may sometimes also cause them to struggle with identifying their sexual orientation or preferences

- **Solar Plexus Chakra:** This centre sits around the upper abdomen and deals with confidence and self – control issues. Its development is usually expected around mid – teenage years and above but they are often affected by controlling relationships which end up causing blockages to result in low self – esteem, self – doubt and lack of confidence

- **Heart Chakra:** This is the centre around the chest area which may also be considered as the centre separating the lower chakras that are mostly involved with physical developments and the upper chakras that may be spiritually related. The centre influences and contributes to the expression of love and compassion. Its developmental stages begin around early adulthood, but the area may be hit by blockages resulting from resentments, loss, and regrets. Such individuals may later tend to keep a closed – heart to prevent themselves from showing empathy or compassion towards others. They may also find it difficult to experience or share love affections with others

- **Throat Chakra:** This centre occupies the throat area to regulate communication and the expression of personal truths. It is expected to peak around mid – adulthood but blockages in the area may cause nervousness and lead to difficulty in expressing or clearly asking for needs to be met. Sometimes it may cause individuals to deprive themselves of speaking up in public domains

- **Third – Eye Chakra:** This centre sits in – between the eyebrows to be affiliated with spiritual messages and intuitive visions. It may also be referred to as the eye of the soul because of its mystical abilities transcending beyond the physical and into the unknown or spiritual realm. It develops naturally through divine guidance and grace but it is mostly expected to peak in adulthood. A closed third – eye chakra may limit the amount of spiritual knowledge and wisdom that may be required to comprehend the mysteries of life

- **Crown Chakra:** This centre sits right on top of the head to establish a direct connection into the spiritual realm for spiritual contact with higher forces of the universe. This level of spirituality may begin at various stages in life, but they are exclusively dictated through divine direction from childhood and up to the peaking stages of adulthood. When this area is not fully developed it tends to limit individuals from accessing higher realms where they could receive and decipher high vibrational messages

Life normally begins at the lowest mind state where a majority of chakra functioning, and intellectual processes may naturally be suppressed. Therefore, mankind often tends to think negatively and make poor judgments about the events in life. This sometimes turn individuals to become mean – spirited and cause misery to fellow humankind due to the lack of sense of reasoning. By this implication mortal human beings may be required to self – improve and have all seven chakras, most especially the heart fully opened to receive good energies from the universe and allow the conscious awareness of God to impact and be practically implemented in the daily activities of their lives.

Discovering Individual Life Plan

Individual life plans are often generated from the date of birth which may reveal life path numbers. This number, once calculated can then be researched to discover further detailed information about;

- The life purpose which may include chosen lessons, the environments, opportunities, and challenges or obstacles that need to be conquered in a particular lifetime for progression onto the next phase. Lessons in the current lifetime often include unfinished lessons or challenges that individuals may have failed to overcome in the previous life. So they are reprogrammed and integrated into the current lifetime to cover an area called the "South node" in the natal birth chart. Once the south node lessons have been completed individuals may now have the chance to progress on to the next level which may be located in the "North node" of the same natal birth chart. Circumstance in south node lessons often ties along with situations causing limitations and hindrances for mortal human beings to live a life of ease. But this may improve and allow mankind to enjoy life again after the south node lessons have been accomplished to allow a progressive shift into the north node where wish fulfilment and enjoyment of life could be realised.

- The information may also describe certain traits and skill sets that an individual may possess from a previous lifetime that could be significant for progression and success in the current lifetime

Finding The Life Path Number And Master Numbers

Life path numbers may be calculated by adding up all the numbers in the date of birth and further broken down to a single – digit number where necessary. For example, if a person is born on 20th February 1992 or 20/2/1992, it will work out as (20+2+1+9+9+2) = **43** or (2+2+1+9+9+2) = **25**, which breaks down to the single digit number (4+3) = **7** or (2+5) = **7**. After the life path number which in this case is seven has been discovered, online research may now be arranged to obtain all the necessary information about the life's mission and purpose for that particular lifetime. Life path numbers also ranges from 1 to 9 and in some instances, they may be accompanied by the master numbers **11, 22,** and **33.**

Master numbers may signify advanced levels in human life experiences. They mostly entail spiritual advancement training for the soul to evolve and prepare to complete the earth's life cycles. These three main master numbers are generally an extension to life path numbers but with extra intensity and emphasis on spiritual advancements that are most essential for old souls who may have completed many life lessons here on earth and are almost ready to ascend into higher levels of consciousness to complete their journey. Discovering master numbers isn't quite easy as finding life path numbers but they may somehow show up in the calculation of life path numbers just before the result is reduced or broken down to a single – digit number or sometimes certain clues from the date of birth may be pieced together with intuitive observation to deduce a certain pattern to confirm the master number. For example, the date of birth above20/2/1992 has twenty (20) as the day of birth and the month of birth = 2. This adds up to get (20+2) = **22.** Though outright the number may resemble a master number it may also require some form of intuitive observation and spiritual discernment to finally confirm whether it is indeed an accompanied master number for this date of birth in that particular lifetime.

Yearly Cycles – Endings And New Beginnings

The nine months period between April to December in astrology may be specifically designed for mankind to go through their various life lessons. It may then be followed by the three months between January and March for testing and review period before the next cosmic year cycle begins with a new set of lessons that must be completed for progression onto the following cycle. Cosmic yearly cycles may also be accompanied by seasonal periods that run through all the twelve zodiac signs with Pisces season which starts approximately around February 20th and ends around March 21st representing a period of completion of the yearly lessons and the end of the twelve seasonal cycles. This then makes way for Aries season which may start from around March 21st to somewhere around April 19th, marking the beginning of a new seasonal cycle.

In spirituality number twelve seems to be a very

significant number in relation to endings or completions of astrological cycles. However, it could also be broken down to the number three to derive other meanings and interpretations. The most common one in esoteric knowledge is the term "Trinity". But in this context, it may refer to the body, mind, and soul in regard to the proper coordination and alignment with the frequency of God to ensure higher spiritual and physical maturity for mortal human beings. Number twelve may also have a strong spiritual bearing because of its affiliation and position as the last on the zodiac wheel which may reinforce and heighten intuition to allow deep mystical abilities.

Generally, all humankind may have a fair share of experiencing and living through all the twelve zodiac signs to gradually develop and enhance their spiritual gifts and talents which may be necessary to successfully navigate through human life and the soul's journey. This inevitable event may also contribute to the heightened spiritual benefits for mortal human beings born under the Pisces sign and those with huge mystical influences of the number twelve in their birth chart. Usually, this collective group of people may classify themselves as old souls who presumably may have lived many lifetimes prior to the current one. Therefore, they must have accumulated a lot of knowledge to understand many big topics and hidden knowledge in spirituality that could unravel some important concepts underpinning the soul's mission. They may also guide fellow humankind to develop some strategic ways to navigate through a lot of the mysteries and secrets in human life.

Divine Gifts

All mortal human beings are born with spiritual gifts, but the application may vary and fall between a separate spectrum of good and bad practices. Meanwhile, it is highly desirable and recommended that mankind may practice and use their gifts for the highest and ultimate good of all humanity. A divine practice or positive use of spiritual gifts may also point to the beginning stages of a spiritual awakening where mankind may try to embrace the higher consciousness of the soul and embody the higher – self. The process may involve divinely guided approaches that may also form part of the natural processes of human evolution. However, it may take several lifetimes for mortal human beings to evolve and reach the level that it could be naturally initiated. But this might seem quite different nowadays because of the amount of knowledge and resources available through modern spirituality which encourages mankind to be in charge of their own destiny and use strong willpower to follow the directives of some essential spiritual exercises and activities to consciously trigger the awakening process.

Reincarnation

It may be a very common practice for souls to be repeating life cycles to clear out old karmic debts and unfinished lessons. They may sometimes be essential for progression unto the advanced spiritual stages to develop good or divine use of spiritual gifts. Meanwhile, reincarnation or the request for another lifetime to complete unfinished lessons is often met with certain delays that may prolong the soul's journey on earth. This could include the waiting periods of finding suitable circumstances and soul groups to join for the next life experiences which may take several human life years after passing on.

Oftentimes, the dynamics in energetic vibration or the differences in life experiences between the old and young soul groups in a lifetime create beneficial circumstances for growth. Because as they mingle, they end up teaching each other some vital lessons to grow and evolve rapidly. But most of the time, the situation causes the minority group which is the old soul group to endure more painful experiences from the vast immature or younger souls who may constantly act out of ignorance. It is usually set up this way in life for old souls to have a chance to heal quicker and clear out karmic debts. Sometimes the experience may also be teaching them important lessons like patience and forgiveness to allow them to balance out their life force energies while the younger ones incur or take a turn to accumulate and develop karmic lessons for their next advancement chapter in life. This may clearly suggest that ignorance may be a big part of the reasons why souls tend to remain bound to earth for a long time until they learn their lessons and get the chance to ascend or exit from the earth's life cycles.

The Sixth Sense

In modern descriptions, divine gifts wrap around the concept of extrasensory perception (ESP) or the sixth sense. They are in some way, shape, or form involved with certain paranormal activities that combine the principles of human sensory organs and substantial use of intuition to perceive spiritual messages and wisdom. Whoever practices them may be inclined with strong spiritual insights and may also have some sort of direct access into the spiritual realm to seek guidance and directives from higher forces to serve humanity. These individuals may include mediums and psychics whose services provide spiritual wisdom that is ideally meant to present the truths needed to elevate human consciousness beyond the basic level of understanding so that the true purpose and involvement of the soul in human life could be well established. But let us also be reminded that although their mission is for the highest good of all humanity there is also an open chance for opposite forces to infiltrate their spiritual practices and cause confusion to reverse the positive intentions. Therefore, it might be of great interest and highly recommendable for individuals to strongly use their own discernment and be extremely vigilant when patronising services of this kind and any other type of spiritual resources.

The list below sheds a brief light on some of the senses that psychics or mediums commonly use in their spiritual practices.

- **Telepathy** – This ability allows individuals to tap into thought processes and establish communication with other individuals without having to use normal sensory channels or through any physical means
- **Clairvoyance** – This ability may also be referred to as "Clear seeing". It involves the ability to see things or images intuitively or mentally. Future events could also be seen with this kind of ability
- **Clairaudience** – This may also be referred to as "Clear hearing" and it gives the ability to intuitively hear voices or spiritual messages
- **Clairsentience** – This involves the ability to intuitively pick up emotional feelings that may be lurking around in an environment. It may also be referred to as "Clear feeling"
- **Claircognizance** – This is the ability to intuitively know something without the chance of prior knowledge or any possible awareness of it previously. It could also be referred to as "Clear knowing"

CHAPTER 4 – BRIEF CONCEPT OF THE TRINITY

A – THE BODY

The body in creation may be classified as a vessel or a means of transport to carry the soul through human life experiences and balance out its scattered energies. From a scientific perspective, the complete makeup of the human body involves a collection of genes that have been passed on from parents to their offspring. Therefore, when a child is born, they are assumed to be carrying twenty – three pairs of various genetic data from the hair to eye colour and sometimes the body type. These inherited genes may also trace far back to generational bloodlines since the inception of the human race. But oftentimes, the genetic information may carry certain bad traits and other negative behavioural patterns that may have been passed on several generations down the line as curses that need to be broken and eliminated to free future generations.

Childhood – Programming

Aside from the inheritance of defective character and behavioural traits, the course and quality of life of an adult human being may significantly be affected by their formative years where various conditioning and programming are heavily picked up. For instance;

- Older members in a child's direct family or the home that they grow up in, may sometimes unknowingly or deliberately influence the child to pick up some unpleasant patterns from their behaviours, experiences, knowledge, traditions, and belief systems which may later instil some unhealthy beliefs and lifestyle choices that may likely lead to disrupt their adult life

- The child's social contact or interaction with the neighbourhood including friendship groups, churches, schools, and the community as a whole may also cause them to adopt many kinds of trendy lifestyles and behaviours which can go a long way to impact their lives either positively or negatively to unexpectedly affect the efficiency of their adult livelihood

- Some children may also experience certain traumatic situations that may register as deep – rooted wounds in their minds and later hunt them in adulthood with unpleasant phobias and fear – based thought patterns that may tend to limit their full potential as an adult. Moreover, some traumatic wounds like co – dependency, people – pleasing, lack of self – worth kind of sabotage, and abandonment issues mostly become so intense that they are often passed on as generational curses

Usually, the childhood stages up to the late teen years may be a crucial moment for mortal human beings to set the foundation right for a healthy adult life experience. This period may hugely contribute to the opening of the first three chakras therefore it may quite be necessary to have these growth stages well defined and influenced by safe societal norms and a healthy home – life conditions that may allow individuals to grow and become independent adults who can fend and secure a responsible life for themselves.

Maintaining The Body Vessel With TLC

The mortal human body could also be considered an aspect and temple of God. Therefore, it may need frequent cleansing and be well maintained in good shape to last a while for the completion of life lessons. Moreover, effective functioning and better management could be achieved by self – assessment, and introspection to spot its own flaws and limitations to allow the right precautions and measures to be taken to heal and improve. This could be anything negative affecting thought patterns, behaviours, and habits that may tend to create imbalances and hold back its full functional operation. The end result could reap benefits like peace and harmony within the individual self which may further extend to improve global human contact and interactions at large.

The gut has a major operation as a secondary source of energy and nutrients for the mortal human body to flourish but it could easily be affected by unhealthy lifestyle choices and bad habits that tend to counteract its positive functional effects and probably leave the body in the worst state possible. Therefore, mankind needs to be careful and watch what they consume whiles also considering moderation before things get out of hand and slip down towards the entrapment of addictions.

Then again, what is being consumed whether edible or mental diet for intellectual purposes must equally be monitored with a reasonable amount to feed or please both the ego – based lower self and the higher self of the spiritual soul. Meanwhile, wiser approaches may be considered to become highly selective and increase the ratio for all the things that positively feed into the embodiment of the higher self more than the highly pleasurable ego – based counterpart for a return benefit of making the body vessel high vibrational to promote longevity. Other recommended efforts to be considered for improvement may include choosing healthy diets and drinking lifestyles that may contribute to individual wellbeing and nourishment. It may also be highly recommendable to incorporate regular exercise regimes to help reduce body fat and cause weight loss to prevent any future health complications that may hinder the enjoyment of life as well as having the body in shape for good looks and high performance.

From The Gut To The Brain

The body functions efficiently with huge support from the circulatory or transport system which relies heavily on the heart. The heart is also assumed to mediate and provide transfer support duties between the brain and gut for the efficient running of the mortal body vessel. Some of the duties of the heart space may somehow be related to the works of the light soul in respect of the feminine influences that it provides to stir up emotions at different density rates to give softer approaches by feeling a way through situations to assist the ego masculine headspace that tends to intellectualise and think through everything before making decisions.

The heart space is also where the heart chakra is located and developed so it might sound quite beneficial to get this energy centre receptive enough to receive high vibrational energies to develop the necessary emotional maturity for effective functioning. The gut in the equation of the heart and brain transfer communication allows the spiritual decoding feature in its makeup to translate intuitive messages into gut feelings to either warn or advise individuals in certain situations. Therefore, for better outcomes from this feature, mankind may want to improve or accelerate the gut's health to a prime condition with herbs, grains, minerals, and clean water.

B – THE MIND

All is the brain and mind because they are true representations of the physical and spiritual nature of the human experience. The brain mainly functions as the central control system that manages various bodily activities ranging from the following procedures;

- Thought formation
- Perception and mindset development
- Decision making
- Emotional release and control
- Motor movements of the body vessel

Thought Formation

Universal life forces transmit energetic information simultaneously to the human brain at various frequency rates. These messages are usually translated by forming thought patterns that allow for conscious analysis to be made with free – will power to arrive at a decision. Consequently, the decisions may also lead to different kinds of actions that may end up with all sorts of outcomes for growth and expansion. This could also be the case of the turnaround events that sometimes arise to detour the original life flow and lead to some uncomfortable routes for life lessons to be learned in an alternative way.

Normal brain function operates between two hemispheres consisting of a left side that deals with analytical or logical reasoning processes and a right side that mainly deals with emotional matters, creativity, and intuitive processes. Meanwhile, the majority of brain processes are mentally developed activities that are managed by the conscious and subconscious minds.

- **The conscious mind:** Mental activities in this area are developed or seen as current thought processes or active responses that may be influenced by instant awareness of the things happening in the surroundings that are in a focal viewpoint. Mankind mostly controls and regulates operations here by exerting individual free – will power to make coherent decisions to implement various actions.

- **The subconscious mind:** This part may act as a storage or data bank that is passively controlled through the psyche for all the involuntary actions and thoughts that have the potential to be brought forward into the conscious mind for analysis and implementation. It is therefore assumed to generate about 90% of the brain's mental faculties which may arrive later in the conscious mind to be assessed with the remaining 10% control power of logical reasoning and physical handling procedures by mortal human beings.

Research may suggest that practicing mindfulness through yoga exercises and meditation may come in handy to reinforce tenacity in cognitive abilities. They may also improve stamina for accuracy and the precision needed for mental activities. Moreso, these techniques often leave a quiescent atmospheric space that tends to decrease the disturbances created by opposing negative forces whose main intentions are to cause distortions during spiritual channelling and when high vibrational messages are being analysed.

C – THE SOUL

Human life consists of matter (the physical human body) and practically the journey of the spiritual soul (Energy) which forms a dual partnership to evolve mortal human beings as it recreates and refines itself for ascension. The design of the human life project allows changes to happen to the human being through a series of life lessons that causes them to outgrow and mature from a lower state of consciousness and evolve into the high vibrational state of consciousness.

The soul's journey normally begins at the dark soul or the egotistical mind state level before gradually advancing with divine guidance and huge support from spiritual guides to shift into the higher consciousness of the light soul. Spiritual guides could be higher forces or the angelic team who could be providing a helping hand and positive influences to counteract any backward movements or stalling caused by the influences of the dark opposing forces and allow human beings to evolve into a higher dimensional state of consciousness. A highly evolved soul may considerably be fully aligned with the body, mind, and the high frequency of God which mostly influences mortal human beings to live a righteous life with love and kindness. This state of being may also focus more on opening the chakras fully to activate positive mannerisms in human habits and behavioural patterns.

CHAPTER 5 - CONCLUSION

When mortal human beings approach the advancing stages of ascension or enter into the spiritual mastery level in the earthly cycles, the creator or higher forces may purposely select and grant those who have through diligent work transmuted and purged out most of the dark low vibrational energies access to higher frequency channels with a calling offer to take on some important roles in the divine workmanship as messengers of the light force to assist in combating the battle of darkness in human life. This stage could be considered as a tipping point in consciousness that respectfully represents true embodiment of the mental frequency of God and a complete opening of the throat, third – eye, and crown chakras which are all essential for the proclamation of the true divine messages to all humankind.

A – THE FREQUENCY OF GOD

Hypothetically, God is a higher frequency state of consciousness that mortal human beings have to evolve to embody. It is also a pure love state of mindfulness that entreats humankind to see past normal flaws and at least see the potential goodness within everybody that could allow **G**oodness **O**verrule **D**arkness all over the world through the understanding of moral excellence. The concept of God generally breeds the essence of having unconditional love for self and for others to allow peace and harmony to reign amongst all humanity. Therefore, mortal human beings may want to gather self – discipline to strictly follow their own path and carry out the necessary improvement work to raise their vibrational frequency higher enough to embrace the principles of God and have it woven all around the aspects of life for better experiences in the world.

What Are The Principles Of God?

God's principles focus on good moral practices through divine love and compassion that allows evil and destructive behaviours that causes harm and misery to others to be rejected. These principles are also capable of dissolving and purging out more negativity to allow the positive changes to transform and make the world a better place for all humanity. A huge advantage of having the human world healed and better transformed is the opportunity that it would allow facilitating the soul's mission for a quick return back home for eternity.

Therefore, now maybe all the moments that we may have to live and make the rightful changes to revamp the old narratives and outdated patterns in human perspectives and routine ways that took away the true meaning and purpose of human existence in creation. This effort would allow humanity to enjoy a breath of fresh air once again in a new world that may be purposely built on the strong pillars of great peace and love.

THE END

Thank you for purchasing this book.

It is my earnest hope that you found the information or content useful enough to help you understand the spiritual topics mentioned in the book. I would also like to apologise for any discrepancies caused as a result of typing errors, omissions, and inaccurate information.

Please if you enjoyed reading the book, kindly leave us a review

Thank you!!...........Love & Light